Rounding It Out

Previous books by Robert Pack

POETRY

The Irony of Joy

A Stranger's Privilege

Guarded by Women

Home from the Cemetery

Nothing but Light

Keeping Watch

Waking to My Name: New and Selected Poems

Faces in Single Tree: A Cycle of Monologues

Clayfeld Rejoices, Clayfeld Laments: A Sequence of Poems

Before It Vanishes: A Packet for Professor Pagels

Inheritance: Reflections on a Gene Pool

Fathering the Map: New and Selected Later Poems

Minding the Sun

POETRY FOR CHILDREN

The Forgotten Secret

Then What Did You Do?

How to Catch a Crocodile

The Octopus Who Wanted to Juggle

ESSAYS AND CRITICISM

Wallace Stevens: An Approach to His Poetry and Thought

Affirming Limits: Essays on Mortality, Choice, and Poetic Form

The Long View: Essays on the Discipline of Hope and Poetic Craft

Rounding It Out
A CYCLE OF SONNETELLES

Robert Pack

THE UNIVERSITY OF CHICAGO PRESS

CHICAGO AND LONDON ☙ ☙ ☙ ☙ ☙

ROBERT PACK taught at Middlebury College in Vermont for thirty-four
years and the Bread Loaf School of English for thirty-one summers as College
Professor of Literature and Creative Writing. For twenty-two years he was director
of the Bread Loaf Writers' Conference. He and his wife, Patty, have moved to
Condon, Montana, where they have built a home in the mountains and where
he now teaches in the English Department of the University of Montana.
He is the author of eighteen books of poetry, including *Fathering the Map:
New and Selected Later Poems* and *Minding the Sun.*

The University of Chicago Press, Chicago 60637
The University of Chicago Press, Ltd., London
© 1999 by Robert Pack
All rights reserved. Published 1999

08 07 06 05 04 03 02 01 00 99   1 2 3 4 5

ISBN: 0-226-64410-3 (cloth)
ISBN: 0-226-64411-1 (paper)

Library of Congress Cataloging-in-Publication Data

Pack, Robert, 1929–
    Rounding it out : a cycle of sonnetelles / Robert Pack.
       p.   cm.
    ISBN 0-226-64410-3 (cloth : alk. paper).
    — ISBN 0-226-64411-1 (pbk. : alk. paper)
    I. Title.
    PS3566.A28R68 1999
    811'.54—dc21   98-35253
                                        CIP

For Erik, Pamela, and Kevin
enlarging the circle

Contents

III *Evening*

IV Night

Acknowledgments

The author wishes to thank the editors of the periodicals in which the following poems were first published:

Academic Questions: "The Little Ones"

The Cream City Review: "Moose," "Suspended Noon," and "Waterfall"

Image: A Journal of the Arts and Religion: "The Aftermath," "A Covenant," and "October Maples"

The New Criterion: "Nothing"

The New Republic: "More Mist"

Raritan: "Pregnant Goat"

Poetry: "Late Summer Purple"

Prairie Schooner: "Counting" and "Inward"

I

Morning

Aubade

Our sun has left just half its life to spill—
About five billion years before it must
Explode, collapse upon itself, and will
Back to the universe its final thrust
Of heat we creatures long have counted on.
Waking warm here in bed, we trust
This light to help imagine when light will be gone
About five billion years from now; it must
Experience diminishment,
As must we too, as must we all.
Observers, we can find our last content
In comprehension that the fall
Of yellow petals on our window sill,
Like little suns, is what we have to will,
A melody to whistle in the dawn:
Our sun has left just half its life to spill.

for Su Tan

3

Invitation

Before you leave, pause here once more with me,
Each one of you alone and one in all,
All merged or each emerging as I see
My storied life in you and call
To you as lover, daughter, wife, or friend,
Approaching through red leaves in dwindling fall
Or vanishing where snow-blown footprints end,
Each one of you alone and one in all.
Son, father, stranger, lives I might have lived,
I summon you within the circle of my mind,
Among the mighty maples I have loved,
To share their shadowed whisperings and find
Acceptance in a reappearing oriole,
Solace in grief when grief is rhymed.
Inheritor of all I love, my memory,
Before you leave, pause here once more with me.

April Dawn

I sing my hungering for green as if I could
Make April luminously greener through
My surging with the sap-inspired wood,
My ice-locked spirit leaping up into
The sun-splashed, hawk-encircled air
As valley vistas blazing in their dew,
Receding and advancing everywhere,
Make April luminously greener through
Dawn's bold unfolded doubling in my sight,
Which knows all dawns like this I've felt before
Because the green I am now singing might
Be everybody's green—it could be your
Repeat reflection on the not yet quite
Completed life we've shared, with more
Loss left to come, more hawk-flight left unseen,
Still hungering for green, more April green.

Silent Dew

When sunlight sparkles in dark crystal dew,
And, kneeling, you discern your image there,
Alone and yet complete, and know
That you can be repeated everywhere
If you look carefully, although
Should you decide to seek me out, to care
Green caring out from your reclusive blue
As, kneeling, you discern your image there,
Would you forsake me for that crystal world
Repeated and complete with only you
To care how carelessly the mind can curl
Back orbiting itself, can turn into
A universe where nothing would be said,
Where blue recedes into still deeper blue,
With your lone image glowing in your head
When sunlight sparkles in dark crystal dew?

Comfort

With precious little left to hope for now
This mid-May morning in warm, hazy sun,
I till the soil to make its grit allow
My hands to fondle in new seeds and stun
Another quickening from inert ground
As if some consolation for me, one
Old stony disbeliever, can be found
This mid-May morning in warm, hazy sun.
But comfort does not mix with consciousness;
My disbelief in any breeding life to live
Beyond what I have here and now is less
Tough than true stone, yet can contrive
Surviving music that can bless
Blank air just as an early bee is bound
For where new blooms will come—to show me how,
With precious little left to hope for now.

Late Summer Purple

Wild aster, bee balm, phlox, chrysanthemum
Proclaim pure purple in the pallid dawn,
Asserting there's more blossoming to come,
More purple in the prickling thistle thorn,
More purple in the valley's swirling haze;
Even the robin's shadow on the lawn,
Even your welcome of the dwindling days,
Proclaim pure purple in the pallid dawn.
Pure purple is the color of your need
To have your mood made manifest, your final flair
Before October's culminating leaves exceed
In parting opulence the purple air
That radiates about your head
As if dispensing rapture everywhere
You move to make a purple hymn to hum:
Wild aster, bee balm, phlox, chrysanthemum.

Lilacs

While merging with each lost, receding May,
Lilac aroma flows out in the dawn
Along the misted field as if to stay
By endlessly departing—as a fawn,
Poised still in fear, then follows her mother,
Leap after longer overarching leap,
Into the underbrush in a brown blur
Too vague for fading memory to keep.
Lilac aroma flows out in the dawn
As if profusion loosened to prolong
Ripe plenitude, as if pink fragrance were not born
To dwindle like the whippoorwill's frail song
Which follows downstream to the underbrush
Where the forgotten watchers play
Among cool ferns, laughing themselves into a hush
While merging with each lost, receding May.

for Woody and Audrey Klein

Moose

Simply to look—and then to see we see
The hemlock and the white pine and the spruce,
Not just the trees as trees, but equally
Their aura of magnificence, the moose
Among them staring as dawn mist delineates
His flat black snout, the beard-like throat-skin bell,
With only his lips moving as he waits
For us to move so he can tell
The hemlock and the white pine and the spruce
From what he makes of us observers there.
And thus between us watchers comes a truce—
A thrill of promise in the parting air
That means whatever eyes exchange—so loose
And liltingly it floats out everywhere
To ask someone to pause, like you or me,
Simply to look—and then to see we see.

for John Elder

Reflections

If you wish to embrace me in the end,
Watching the silver mist swirl in the dawn
And surge up from curved valley hills which send
Reflected light in brightened shadings born
Of their own undulating hues that flare
To bluer brightenings, pause here
This morning as I wait upon a rock and stare,
Watching the silver mist swirl in the dawn.
Look for me where plump mushrooms nudge up through
The forest mulch, my pale inheritors, and where
The woodpecker attacks his pulpy tree, or you
Can seek me where two streams converge
To swell a beaver pond, for I will hold my blue
Reflections in the mist until you merge
Into mild autumn in my mind and blend
With my wish to embrace you in the end.

More Mist

Your backward glance still unaccounted for,
This lingering of misty morning light
Adds more mist where already there was more,
Making smooth hills and sky merge in my sight,
Making me once again relive the day
You walked through that green gateway to the sea
As if intending just to visit, not to stay,
As if your drowning could be shared with me.
This lingering of misty morning light
Swirling above the hills, churns the blown sky
Into a surging sea; within my sight
I merge with you and cannot tell which I is I,
The I remaining or the I that's gone,
As some remembered whippoorwill sings on
Inside the mist that breeds more mist and more
With your last backward glance still unaccounted for.

Dewdrop

One dewdrop gliding down a maple leaf,
Observed as I observe myself observing it,
Must speak for me my still unspoken grief
Now that you're packed down in a hillside pit
As if transplanted like a startled tree,
Another silver maple that can fit
This grove contrived for symmetry,
Observed as I observe myself observing it.
And if I lean in close enough to see
The neighborhood of leaves reflected there
In one inclusive drop, bowing like me,
Poised to evaporate in morning air
Where once I used to watch the driven bee
Dally in drunken summer everywhere,
Can one diminished image soothe my grief—
One dewdrop gliding down a maple leaf?

Ripeness

Familiar summer now seems strangely new
As this faint chill of languid August dawn
Shivers the clustered berries in the dew
As if completed ripeness has been born
From ripeness recollected ripening,
Ripeness again repeated, here and gone,
Presence and loss together as both bring
A scented chill to languid August dawn.
Five billion years of evolution on our earth
Produced this momentary ripeness in the sun,
This rounded revelation at the birth
Of sweet acceptance in the fruitful one
Prolific meaning earth can offer you,
Ripeness to smell, to taste, to meditate upon,
Red raspberries becoming redder in your view
Which makes familiar summer strangely new.

II

Midday

A Covenant

When I first courted you, how could I know
Why you would linger watering each vegetable?
Slowly the summers passed from frost to snow,
Then suddenly the children were not there, an owl
Remaining as their moonlit afterglow.
The faint tang of tomato on my tongue
Is all the harvest in late haze to tell
Why you would linger with each vegetable.
Now June returns, you're growing young
By watering the garden once again,
Imagining the children went away
To make a seasonal return—just when
Is still uncertain, though you watch the way
The arc of droplets pauses in the sun,
Weaving white light into a rainbow show
As when I courted you and could not know.

Pruden's Purple

How, Pruden's Purple, O my luscious one,
O indeterminate, will you appear?
Since my imprudent love searching began,
I've lusted for you, kept you here
Smack on my lips and tongue, a breath away
Within the garden of my memory
Where squash and stationary eggplants stay
Predictably in shape as appetite can see.
O indeterminate, will you appear,
So densely sprawling like an aging bush,
Your shadow might be taken for a bear,
So leafy-thick, so languorously lush,
Impenetrable even to a passing bee,
Your ruby treasure will be hidden there
Still undetected by the spying sun,
Pruden's, tomato, O my luscious one?

Suspended Noon

Now shadowless beside the silent lake,
The pause of noon suspends you as you are—
As if for one held moment you forsake
All memory; not even hope can mar
Absorption in the body so complete:
Soft warmth of sunlight on your hair,
The shudder of chilled water on your feet.
The pause of noon suspends you as you are
And, as you are, now shadowless and still,
An apparition carved from radiance,
Emptied of all desire, with nothing left to will,
Beyond ancestral randomness and chance,
You stir in me a sudden need to break
The brittle stillness of your trance
In time to rescue muted time and shake
A hint of shadow from the loon-stirred lake.

Pregnant Goat

Aware that I am here observing her,
The pregnant, brown goat browsing in that field
Now pauses at her chewing as the whir
Of swallows swooping from the barn, the peel
And splatter of their twitterings, accompany
Wild flapping of her ears, although
From my side of the road, how can I know
If the connections I see she can see?
The pregnant, brown goat browsing in that field
Appears serene to me; perhaps it's true
She takes raw pleasure in the pleasure yield
That I conceive from watching her, as if she knew
She has more life inside her life, more time,
As she seems roused to feel the stir
Of her slow browsing in my blood when I'm
Aware that I am here observing her.

Waterfall

You cup the leaping water in both hands,
Kneeling beside the spuming waterfall,
And what your untried body understands,
Poised in pure receptivity, is all
That childhood can allow, sensation so
Harmonious—the stream, the flute-trill call
Of orioles—you know by knowing not to know,
Kneeling beside the spuming waterfall.
And I can merge with you but only by
Withholding what this father wishes most—
To touch, to keep, as if by touching I
Might pour out of myself, a ghost
Of foam and spray, a floating shade who has
New spuming flow to voice my soft demands.
But no, I have no touch to keep you as
You cup the leaping water in both hands.

Gifted

To feel my blood's inheritance in you,
My son, congenial laughter to go on
By going on when others' goings are long gone,
Cast out grim need of greedy purpose to pursue
More meaning than mere mortal laughter will allow
And let the vigor in your muscled shoulders try
Through work to ease your body so it can endow
Cold nights with temporary rest untroubled by
The uncongenial endings daylight must go on
Enduring to go on with work. Let your skilled hands
Revive the grainy eloquence of wood
For what a home and household understands
Of daily living, of work's brave, ongoing good,
With just a pause of laughter left to dwell upon,
Before forgetting, as survivors all must do,
My laughing blood's inheritance in you.

Your Name

With almost nothing left except your name,
Faintly I still can re-envision you
Emerging naked from sea surging blue,
Your breasts illuminated with the same
Pale, phosphorescent glow that flared
Up pulsing in one overwhelming spew
As if a sunken city flourished there.
Though I can re-envision you
With white, forsaken arms stretched out
To summon me, could I have known
I would abandon what now seems just pure
Reflection that you wove from spume-glow blown
Into a hazy spray? The ocean's lure
Was irresistible; why should I blame
The blur of tidal foam for making me forget
With almost nothing left except your name?

Butterfly Beatitude

The butterfly alights upon cow dung;
It flutters there, my dear, for you to see
Delicate colors on display among
Bare blazing heaps. Delighting in such irony,
Conjoining high and low, combining dry and wet,
Crude comeliness appears to me
Its raison d'être in the field—and yet
It flutters there, my dear, for you to see.
It migrates to New England in the spring,
Depositing its eggs (as you might guess)
And back again to Florida to bring
Its destiny full circle in the fall.
If there were further happiness
For butterflies beyond mere reproduction, all
Its insect soul would wish is this refrain be sung:
The butterfly alights upon cow dung.

Scorpion Flies

We've seen the likes of this—it's déjà vu,
I mean the courtship of hot scorpion flies:
He brings a nuptial insect meal in order to
Entice his chosen one to copulate; he tries
To hold her there, gripping the tasty bait
Until his love load is deposited.
This is true purpose in the body's fate—
I mean the courtship of hot scorpion flies.
If nuptial food runs out, she will depart
Before his mission is complete, but if instead
Some morsel still remains, they'll start
Domestic life with a fine fight—a kind
Of property debate, just the prelegal part.
And thus a slight resemblance comes to mind,
Perhaps of him with me and her with you.
We've seen the likes of this—it's déjà vu.

First Frost

The first full frost of autumn—it is here,
Its implications quiver in the boughs
Still laden with late summer leaves as deer,
Astonished at frost's sudden whiteness, now
Peer from the pulp-strewn, hemlock-shaded woods
While wondering what universal white might mean,
What winter broodings and what winter moods,
Transformed from June's illuminated green.
With deer's eyes I perceive annihilation there
Beneath this filigree of loveliness,
This lace of little markings everywhere
Frost touches with white delicate finesse.
Its implications quiver in the boughs
As if to give assurance to hope's guess
Some sly design of preservation will appear
Now with the first full frost of autumn here.

for Julia Alvarez

October Maples

No wind at all, late golden maples glow
Silent and still in bold October sun,
And I, contained within their aura, know
Their luminescent stillness to the bone, at one
With silence made articulate as light,
At one with your own oneness even though
I see myself dissolving in your sight.
Silent and still in bold October sun,
The windless lake reflects the maples' glow,
And I—as if my mind becomes the lake—
Know only what its open waters know,
The oneness of its give and take
Of noonday light; passing October pauses
On the lake of my still mind, without a cause,
And where there stirs no fluting sound, no flow,
No wind at all, late golden maples glow.

Baled Hay

Wheels of baled hay bask in October sun:
Gold circles strewn across the sloping field,
They seem arranged as if each one
Has found its place; together they appeal
To some glimpsed order in my mind
Preceding my chance pausing here—
A randomness that also seems designed.
Gold circles strewn across the sloping field
Evoke a silence deep as my deep fear
Of emptiness; I feel the scene requires
A listener who can respond with words, yet who
Prolongs the silence that I still desire,
Relieved as clacking crows come flashing through,
Whose blackness shows chance radiance of fire.
Yet stillness in the field remains for everyone:
Wheels of baled hay bask in October sun.

for Richard and Len Rubin

III

Evening

The Unspoken

If you agree to meet me by the lake,
If you say what I've dreamed I heard you say,
Can I respond, reach out, and break
The desiccated silence that submerged my way
And kept unspoken words still sunken there,
Cramped in my mind; can I now reinvent,
Out of the muck, the humid, storm-inducing air,
A sound more sinewy than merely sighed content
If you say what I dreamed I heard you say?
And now gray rains arrive, drenching the ferns
Along the willow-shaded shore, scrubbing rough hues
Of mossy rocks so they reflect red light that turns
Dense purple, pauses, darkening to clay;
Can that pause summon from the bottom ooze
A turtle's gold, all-speaking eyes which gape awake,
If you agree to meet me by the lake?

Swimmer

I'm summoned from my reverie where I return
Across the lake, stroke after lilting stroke,
Each drop from my arched arm a sun-spun urn
Reflected in late orange light, and wake
To where I am, still flowing with the homeward tide,
Still bobbing with the water's buoyancy.
Smooth as the easy, breeze-rubbed air, I glide
Across the lake, stroke after lilting stroke,
And each time I awaken, I'm still here—that's me
Still coasting with my undiminished pull,
My feet slowly aflutter as if I
Could ride this drowsy rhythm in the lull
Before blurred shadows seal the purple sky,
Content in this eternity of swimming free
And homeward still before I wake to learn
My summoning comes too late to return.

Body Praise

Meanwhile I'll celebrate each body part,
The noble nose that boldly leads the way,
Gray eyes that glisten with seduction's art,
The mouth whose smile tilts subtly on display,
For what am I if not the aggregate
Of my proud appetites, the nervous leap
Of gossip from each synapse to relate
Its story to the neural neighborhood and keep
The noble nose that boldly leads the way
Directed toward a transcendental goal
To justify pained searching some redeeming day.
So thanks, dumb feet, thighs, genitals, you all
Have something to contribute, gut and heart,
And though you cannot glimpse beyond that wall
Where all the great conclusions start,
I'll celebrate you, meanwhile, body part.

September

It's brash September once again, I'm here
Outside myself, with no temptation to return,
Suspended in a calm devoid of fear,
And nothing somber left to learn
Except what I have learned before—
Pine needles on the umber forest floor.
Ecstatic air sustaining me
Outside myself, with no temptation to return,
Why should I circle back to see
Pine needles on the umber forest floor,
Cascading geese across the sky,
And by the garden gate, your silhouette?
Now peering down the dwindling valley, I
Perceive where merged hills halt hazed light, and yet
I needn't speculate beyond, my dear,
It's brash September once again, you're here.

Leaves in Autumn Wind

You need no meaning more than mindless leaves
That brush their reds and yellows in bright air
As if to specify an image there
Whose disappearance can be rendered permanent;
Thus with their vanishing contained, you grieve
So quietly that it might seem you spent
Whatever sorrow might inform the scene,
Leaves brushing reds and yellows in bright air,
On finding meaning merely in what colors mean.
I still can see you underneath a tree,
Your hands outstretched to catch more evening light,
Though maybe in your mind you're watching me,
And maybe meaning means no more than sight
Can cherish, and in cherishing let be,
So that for all your minding you believe
You need no meaning more than mindless leaves.

Fish Story

Consider the fulfilled, blue-headed wrasse,
His gaudy fins resplendently displayed
Among his paramours, and watch him pass,
As if alone he constituted a parade,
Before his harem's drab, admiring multitudes,
Undifferentiated but for size.
The largest female picks him as her prize,
His gaudy fins resplendently displayed,
Knowing her chance will come, since when he dies,
She'll turn the ultimate, genetic trick
By metamorphosing into a male—
A hormone's feat providing a much needed prick
To mundane sexual imaginings that pale
Before bold his/her breedings of more his/her broods.
So if your life's a marital morass,
Consider the fulfilled, blue-headed wrasse.

Painting a Bird

All that remains for me is to refuse
Green leaf-light there by conjuring a ruby bird
In a red bush of many reds that I can choose
Beneath a crimson sky—reds random and absurd,
Invented as assertions of my mind
And woven in a tapestry with purple trees
Along an orange stream, so I can find
Myself—a figure sapphire blue, who sees
Fused redness there by conjuring a ruby bird.
For what has brutal nature's brush contrived
That I should imitate her summer atmosphere,
Her cornstalk green that has again survived,
Green of renewal not for me? Only green fear
Of dying, blaring in my head like bees,
Green hillside shadows darkening to blue,
Remain of red refusal I in vain refuse!

The Vortex

I glimpse the blue jay and the kingfisher
About to merge within my view,
Knowing this flattened evening light can blur
My sense of depth and lead me back into
A fire-lit cave where all I see
Are images that flutter on a wall:
Two deer beside a stream, beneath a tree,
A fox attending to another fox's call.
About to merge within my view,
A circle that might represent the moon
Appears as if it is preparing to
Rise through its stone-set orbit so that soon
It will eclipse, with just the slightest cosmic stir,
A circle that might represent the sun,
Until emerging from the vortex of this blur
I glimpse the blue jay and the kingfisher.

for Mark Strand

Inward

November murmurings, November sighs,
As bare wind bends the emptied maple bough
And autumn's last exuberance replies
By gripping inward, gripping down, and now
Slow drowsy wasps below the dusky eaves,
Wavering in blue wafted chimney smoke
Entomb themselves in their clay-brittle hives
Whose silence summons as if silence spoke.
As bare wind bends the emptied maple bough
And deer dash through the unprotecting field
Circled by startled crows, I wonder how,
By sinking further inward, I can yield
What death requires and yet hold on to grieve
Lament's oncoming lullaby. Alive, I'm still alive,
There's stirring chill life left in me to prize
November murmurings, November sighs.

for Paul Mariani

39

Our Kind

November drizzle freezes in the firs.
The carcass of a disemboweled buck
Sways from a neighbor's rope and stirs
Fantasies of escape and luck,
Though fear strikes home that humankind
Murders more when there are more of us,
And we're increasing faster now; we're not designed
To live too close together. And it's close—
The carcass of a disemboweled buck—
It's close to where my neighbor's pine grove bleeds
Right into mine, and closer in my mind
Which shares his acrid wind. I only find
Cold consolation in how hunger feeds
Indifferently: our kind's not kinder than their kind—
Rodent incisors, talons, thorns and thistle burrs.
November drizzle freezes in the firs.

Heron

So stick-like still, I might not notice him,
Perched on a bleached-out stretch of sunken tree
Protruding like a respite from the stream,
Until he lifts his purplish head so I can see
He has my thoughts in mind—he watches, he's alive,
Perhaps perceiving kindred stillness here in me,
Silent across the stony stream's divide,
Perched on a bleached-out stretch of sunken tree.
Pleasure of merely peering at a living thing
Wells up in me as if this moment was
Appointed for the heron there to bring
Me to my senses, make me pause to gaze
Through thickened evening light and dim
Congested shadows on the stream's blown haze,
As inward silence grips me, gray and grim,
So stick-like still I might not notice him.

The Aftermath

Nothing remains except the aftermath—
Odor of rain, now that the valley air is dry,
A hint of whispering along the forest path
That we once wandered through here, you and I,
As if past presence lingers through the pantomime
Of muted loss, rehearsals of good-bye
With more ongoing aftermath to come:
Odor of rain, now that the valley air is dry.
And if no one returns to realize
That we are gone, and no one anywhere—
On hearing how the startled blackbird cries—
Can conjure our late absence waiting there
From the light scent left over from the storm,
Who will distinguish in mild evening air
Cosmic indifference from cosmic wrath?
Nothing remains except the aftermath.

IV

Night

The Little Ones

Who will protect the little ones at night
When black winds dagger down the mountain pass,
Ice grips the staggered trees and mighty
February occupies the fields? The mass
Of hunkered snow heaps boulder high
And higher onto more unfathomable snow,
Leaving no constellations there to chart the sky
When black winds dagger down the pass.
And when the big ones come, row after row,
How can I help, how can I even try
To help, and where, for god's sake, will I be
After the marching big ones do
What black winds do, unheeding as the sea
That swallows everything it breeds? And who
Has husbanded his strength to rend things right?
Who will protect the little ones at night?

Vistas

Despite unswerving joy of having loved
Blue vistas rising from half-misted peaks,
White birches glowing in a hemlock grove,
Silent across crisp moonlit snow
A gliding owl, a rabbit dangling from its beak,
Reminds me how quenched hungers go
Right back to being hungers once again.
Blue vistas rising from half-misted peaks,
Foam clouds receding like froth ocean tide,
Release me from my gnawing inwardness
Where still raw losses and regrets reside;
I laugh out loud my universal YES,
Impersonal and everlasting, then
I press my knuckles hard against my eyes.
I cannot let that rabbit go ungrieved
Despite unswerving joy of having loved.

for Stanley and Virginia Bater

Stone Thoughts

I speak cold silent words a stone might speak
If it had words or consciousness,
Watching December moonlight on the mountain peak,
Relieved of mortal hungers, the whole mess
Of needs, desires, ambitions, wishes, hopes.
This stillness in me knows the sky's abyss,
Reflected by blank snow along bare slopes,
If it had words or consciousness,
Would echo what a thinking stone might say
To praise oblivion words can't possess
As inorganic muteness goes its way.
There's no serenity without the thought *serene*,
Owl-flight without spread wings, honed eyes,
    hooked beak,
Absence without the meaning *absence* means.
To rescue bleakness from the bleak,
I speak cold silent words a stone might speak.

Because

Because the cougar cracks the antelope,
Because the weak hawk chick's pushed from its nest
To spare scarce meat that nourishes the strong,
Because we kill for love and food, I place blind hope
In blind, impersonal acceptance of all wrong,
Knowing remorse can lacerate the breast
Of those who'd redesign their hungry wills
Because the weak hawk chick's pushed from its nest.
Nature's serene indifference is a curse
Only to those who fail to feel sublimity
In transformations of late light that spills
On purple mountains or green frothing sea,
Mindless magnificence, and, worse,
Demanding some redeeming purpose kills
The dazed beholder's blazing joy, and kills blind hope,
Because the cougar cracks the antelope.

Our Forefathers

Must I still sing a song of massacre?
They needed space and food, the brave who dared
To immigrate to North America,
Who killed all mammoth and all short-faced bear.
And then saber-toothed tigers were all gone,
Wild horses and wild camels disappeared,
Exterminated by our ancestors, each one,
Without memorials, without a tear
For the unwary sloth, the mastodon,
And still they needed space, the brave who dared.
More living species keep on going down
Despite our gift of the capacity to care,
Though always in contention with our own,
Ravaging and consuming everywhere.
Hard to believe such killing has and does occur,
So I must sing my song of massacre.

Acid Rain

Bleak acid rain conceives of emptiness,
The vanishing of everything we love,
Green plants, green trees, the whole proliferating mess
Of flashing fish below, bright birds above,
Surmising that extinction will be caused by us
Before the destined bursting of our sun
Brings down the big demise to one
And all who tread the earth; and thus
The vanishing of everything we love
Would consummate what replication had begun
In some warm pond, without a respite we can find
For peace in human time through what we think.
Whether we look ahead or look behind,
We see a void; we've brought creation to the brink,
And since there's nothing further to confess,
Bleak acid rain conceives of emptiness.

Nothing

If knowing I know nothing comforts me,
That out of nothing sudden space commenced
In time to cool and bring forth stars, a galaxy
To mother us and call our own, immense
By our brief human lights, and yet just one
Rotating structure among multitudes,
Then who will notice nothing when we're gone;
Can nothing comfort when there's no one left to brood
That out of nothing cooling space commenced?
Perhaps some enterprise beyond our need
For solace in the face of nothing might be sensed
In nature's unrelenting laws which heed
No animal or human cry, some yet to be
Vast consciousness, for which I am the seed,
Nurtured from nothing by the light of stars to see
If knowing I know nothing comforts me.

Numbered

Numbered among blurred multitudes of stars,
Each burning to fulfill its fated role
As red dwarf or white giant or black hole,
I recognize my heritage from Mars,
God of grim war whose cycling has foretold
Uncounted stories, ruling the fixed sphere
Of my self-dread, my unrelenting fear,
Still burning to fulfill its fated role.
News from the night arrives right here,
Reviving old regrets as you appear
Among the Pleiades now blazing in my head
Along with comets sighing my desire
That blink out in the dark above my bed—
And you are gone, although I still conspire
To seize you, orbiting with iron Mars,
Among blurred multitudes of numbered stars.

Friends

Alive among the multiplying dead,
Laughter of friends, lilting inflections of
Their silver-tongued replies, what can be said
That might appease my unaccepting love
So recollection of past laughing happiness
Does not sweep present happiness away?
Is loss at last composed of words of loss
Now the lost past has settled in to stay,
Laughter of friends, lilting inflections of
Their moonlit voices in the maple leaves,
In leaping waters of a stream above
Smooth stones—a congregation that believes
Nothing remains and nothing that is said
Can grieve the way remembered laughter grieves?
I'm still alive with laughter in my head,
Alive among the multiplying dead.

for Bob Hill

Counting

How long since I last counted can it be
Before you'll have to live alone—
Just you, the dogs, and that protecting willow tree
Planted when we moved here, when stone by stone
We cleared the tangled field and built the wall
That circled in our lives? So count on me,
Though numbered words now guard this moonlit house,
While, staring at the fire, you hear the call
Across the hemlock dark of owls who see
Small tell-tale stirrings in the grass,
Before you'll have to live alone,
Before the wall we crafted stone by stone
Goes creeping back into a weed-strewn field.
Will that old willow serve as company
The night my pond gleams like a fallen shield?
How long since I last counted can it be?

for Patty

Leave-Taking

So good-bye body, good-bye universe,
Its nearing time to take your leave of me,
Although desire's not spent yet to converse
With you, nor lost is curiosity
About your chance appearance on the cosmic scene
Or how complex became complexity,
Whose meaning meant what need contrived to mean
In time to take untimely leave of me.
Can solace yet be found for one who grieves
A father lost, a mother vanishing,
In just low oceanic choiring of blown leaves,
Encounters of a swallow's wing
With orange evening light, no more, no less?
Yes, there's sufficient reason still to sing
A rounded song for better or for worse,
So good-bye body, good-bye universe.

Nocturne

How little separates me from the night:
My moist breath merges with the moistened air;
From my cupped hands a flutter of reflected light
Ascends as if a bird had been enfolded there—
A gathered whiteness that can fly
My message of replenished care,
My offer to the dark, my sole reply.
My moist breath merges with the moistened air,
Summons to its blurred self what waits beyond,
Projects its own illumination to
Moon-laden branches by the frozen pond,
To cavern icicles our awed ancestors knew.
I see how cloudy indivisibility
Divides, how whirled division mists to white;
I recognize lulled voices calling me,
How little separates me from the night.